I0489809

Live your dream and love your life

Live your dream and love your life...

LOVE AND LIFE
Live your dream and love your life...

Copy Right

First Edition: February 2023

Info about Edmarys Menendez

Email:
edmarys.menendez@yahoo.com

Edited in USA

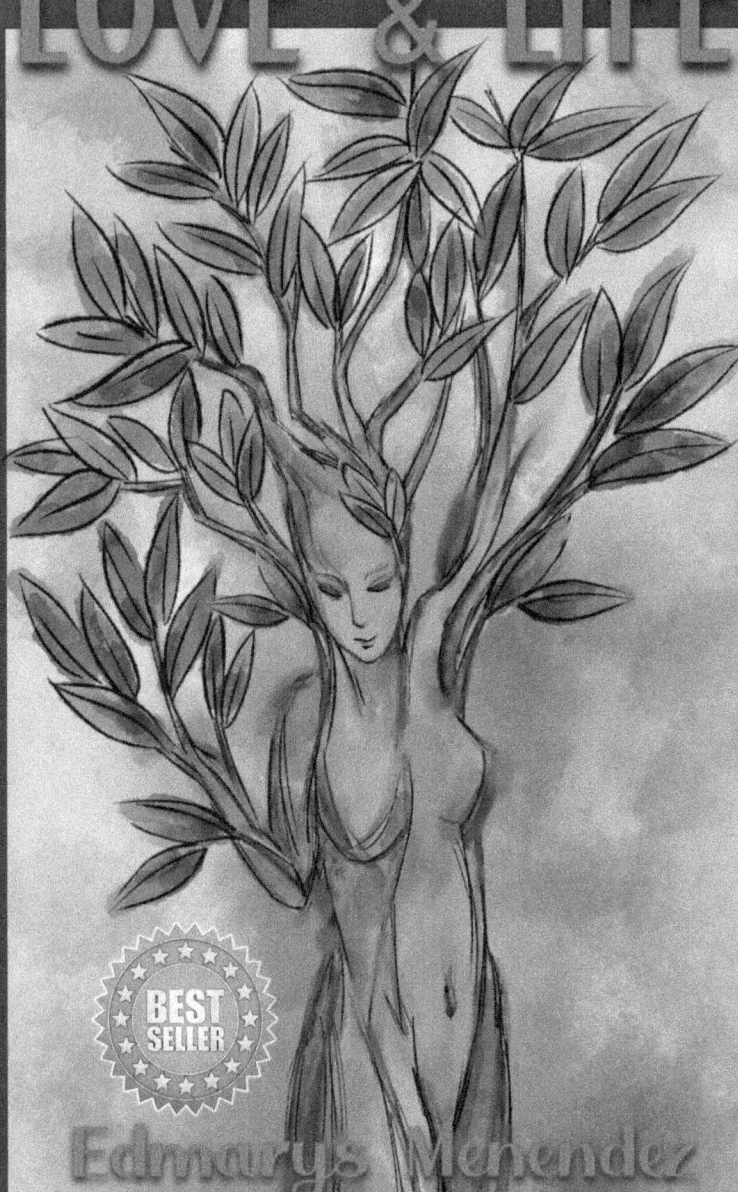

LOVE & LIFE

BEST SELLER

Edmarys Menendez

Dedication:

I dedicate this book to my great grandmother
Cruz Maria Torres
and my grandmother
Margarita Ruiz.
I also dedicate it to my family who have supported and loved
me since my life began.
Nothing is more powerful than the love and support of your
loved ones...
your blood, the ones who stick by you no matter what
circumstances.
To those who aren't also family but have been there as well.
Thank you for your infinite support and inspiring me to share my
love with the world with a single pen stroke.
Here is to you all.

My Lovely Cruz...

Live your dream and love your life

The Matriarch:

Great grandmother of mine,

Spirited and positive as can be,

The strongest in our family,

Standing with 96 and can still see.

Hard worker since age 09,

Always cooking for the young,

Her delicious steaks,

Watering our tongues.

Constantly there when needed,

As amazing daughter & loving mother,

Magnificent granny and great granny,

Simply extraordinary like no other.

She fills my life with joy,

Included with courage and hope,

Without her I cannot live,

She started the family rope.

Present since I first saw light,

© Edmarys Menendez ©

With a smile from ear to ear,

A purple flower on her hair,

Full of happiness in her eyes with tears.

Her unique smell of roses,

Blissfully flowing in odorless air,

While soothing dreadful vibes,

A magical ability so rare.

I'm blessed and thankful of my dear Cruz,

A compassionate and humble old lady,

Who influenced me to love and appreciate,

The one who I'll remember when I have my baby.

Prologue:

Some say in order to survive you need a career or a "title." We all have activities and hobbies that soothe us. But who's to say you will end up being that so called somebody? All you know is that your career will consist of delighted moments and pleasant memories that follow. Now you can say that is all you are aiming for. Being around those you love and love you brings you joy. Spreading and sharing your happiness with others also brings you joy. So if someone ever asks you what your career will be in the future, you will say, a joy bringer. You will motivate, up-lift, and guide those in need no matter their struggles as you do now.

As of this moment, you can say you've been quite useful to several people that have come across your life. By this rate, you will end up being an outstanding citizen needed in every community. Exchanging genuine smiles, this is what you do. You create positive liveliness and glee in the most colorless and gloomy span of time. There is no need to say how tough this career can be. Sometimes the outcome isn't what you expected. Nonetheless, there's no way in finding out if you don't take risks in giving your all, at least in this case to support others.

Those who ask if you know what you're doing, simply answer with a yes. You will complain at the end of the day, exhausted from giving a helping hand to some who don't acknowledge or even accept your help. Yet, every morning you wake, a tiny spec of bright light will seem to shine from your eyes. Your lips will part in smiles and smirks and that organ we all have in between our upper ribcage, behind our chest, well it will throb in ways you cannot think possible. It is a bit cliché to say that an act of kindness not only elevates the spirits of those we help. It fills you with hope and that is immensely accurate. You will love what you do and you will keep doing it as a career. Though, you do need a break at times. Too much of something can turn into something appalling. Your profession is to be an encourager. That is what you are. But not only to others, to yourself as well. As you read this book, this is what you will gain. When you are done with it, pass it along and encourage the rest to do the same.

Live your dream and love your life

Table of Contents:

Love Poems

Life Poems

© Edmarys Menendez ©

Life Writings

In Between

Your Conscience

Lover

Learn To Move On

The Thirst

Distinctiveness

The Hidden Soul

Love Writings

Rise

Third Love

Hopeless Romantic

Motherly Hand

Self-Love

The Art Within

Love is Life

Live your dream and love your life

To love is to live...

© Edmarys Menendez ©

The Famous Question:

You are a God.

Infallible is what you define.

Adrenaline rush through my veins.

Powerful body connections.

A soothing melody in my heart, filled with monstrous and vociferous explosions of passionate romance.

An inundation of an unexplainable emotion unable to circumvent.

Cohesive with great sanction in the mind, heart, and physical world.

You are the one.

Positive feelings intensified with pure and perfect truths of the pumping organ inside oneself.

I am now embellished with his robust trusting words.

Superfluous sadness relegated to the dark allies of the tempting and grievous monster.

But you bolster me.

Inquisitive I once was to find what now lies in between my arms.

I fly in high levels of a different world with you.

What I now have was once nebulous in my eyes.

New eyesight as you entered into my life.

Time is depreciated since it's now eternal.

No ending of this.

Live your dream and love your life

It's a wall of exciting stimulation provided with a protected shield of a tenet.

Have I now realized this elongated explanation is in fact the phrase everyone wants to experience?

It is to my knowledge, discretions, and experience that I have discovered the famous question.

Am I in love?

© Edmarys Menendez ©

What You Do:

Your touch, your warmth, your grasp, your stare, your lips, your sweetness...

It's what you do to me.

An unfamiliar feeling; indescribable. Is this love? This, us, I cannot describe. The feeling is extraordinary.

It's what you do to me.

Your touch. Oh my. My insides move with delight. So lively, it's unreal.

It's what you do to me.

Your warmth. Woah. My spine weakens and I cannot move. My heart; it's racing.

It's what you do to me.

Your grasp. Oh yes. Those exquisite hand entanglements. Your firm grab on my cheeks as we face together.

It's what you do to me.

Your stare. Ah! It carries so much energy. It's contagious. I am burning inside each second you look into my soul. So addicting I cannot look away.

It's what you do to me.

Your lips. Yes. So soft yet so alive in every kiss. An electric sensation in every connection.

It's what you do to me.

Your sweetness. Lord. Exquisitely perfect. It is out of this world, not humanlike at all. This love is what I crave. You feed me by the second. Such hungriness in my veins. In love is nonsense. This is far beyond anything real, it's our own incredible feel.

It's what you do to me.

The Wanting:

The want of your touch, warmth, and affection.

Strident; agonizing in all steps possible.

A reminder in every swallow, nauseating by hour,

I avert the beastly plunder of my innocence.

I starve from lack of authenticity,

The absence of infatuation in your heart,

I starve promises and a conclusive for an unblemished future,

I crave the unquestionable tries for something beautiful.

I crave valid lips and honest stares,

The soul, incapable to your indefectible physique,

I crave all the shades of your darkness,

And I run impulsively, inhaling this lie,

Searching for more, from your numbed humanity,

Like a monstrous living thing in an unknown habitat.

Empty:

I thought I wouldn't eat,

I thought I wouldn't sleep.

Yet I swallow every piece,

Of bread,

And all tension I release.

Well-fed in bed.

I thought my mind would shut down.

I thought my heart would only frown.

Yet no sign of a breakdown,

Ever appears.

And the beat in my chest slowdowns.

Eyes dry and I cannot hear.

But I have a feeling.

There's something wrong.

He is always back kneeling,

At me where he belongs.

I thought I was fine,

I thought I wasn't blind.

© Edmarys Menendez ©

Yet it's only past nine,

Here at home.

And I want to hide,

In my house alone.

I thought I was in control.

I thought his heart I stole.

Yet empty is my soul,

Since I woke.

And I'm no longer whole;

My heart is broke.

But now it is midnight.

My anguish has vanished.

Hours pass and it is daylight.

I am no longer damaged.

However, I was affected,

Though not by much.

I can say it's what I expected,

But life is non-such.

Because there's so many moments,

No matter how distraught.

Live your dream and love your life

I take a shot,

Since most of those moments can be fought.

Unanswered Questions:

Why?

You don't understand.

Everything you did.

Everything you showed.

Everything you let go of.

Everything you adjusted to.

Everything you put your heart and soul to...

It hurts.

It's like everything you do now has no purpose.

You just do things to do them.

To please others and not yourself.

What happened to you?

No, the question is, why did this happen to you?

You are so confused, so lost, and so aggravated.

You don't understand why this happened.

Live your dream and love your life

The desire to do things has disappeared in midair.

Laziness has become more of your personality than a trait.

Your heart blew up into millions of pieces that night, and you don't know what to do anymore.

Your body is at every place it needs to be as your daily routine continues.

But your heart, oh your heart, it has taken your mind to another path.

It glued itself to the destination this path led to and now you're stuck.

Stuck of how uncontrollably painful this has become.

Frustration, tears, anger, want...so many emotions and you don't know what to do with them.

You are in so much pain and you can't let go.

Why is this so painful?

Why did it have to happen with that certain individual?

Why did you fall so hard?

Why did you rush it all?

Why did you trust so easily?

You have so many questions and no answers.

You're so drawn to those past memories, the good ones.

Every breath reminds you of a specific moment, every blink

reminds you of a specific gesture, and every moment in your

body reminds you of a specific second, where your insides felt

an explosion of incredible unexplainable feelings.

You just noticed your need.

Oh no, why is this happening?

Why did it have to be with that person?

Why is this so aggravating?

Why must we all go through these rough patches in our lives?

Why must they hurt so much?

You start thinking the more painful these challenges get, the
stronger you become.

Or are you wrong?

Are you just assuming that everything will be okay?

What if it won't be?

What if you become aloof to all existence?

Your mind thinks one way and your heart thinks another.

Live your dream and love your life

You don't know whether to pretend like nothing happened or cry out loud and let the world know how you feel or whether to deal with it and realize that this will happen several more times in your life.

Sometimes you are afraid and truly afraid.
You feel isolated, inexperienced, and innocent...
But there are other times where you feel a sense of power.
You gain courage, wisdom, and a desire to love.

Why is it so mesmerizing?

You crave that love.
It is something you cannot hide.
It can have its advantages but it can also have its drawbacks.

Why must this broad topic be so convoluted, so tangled, such a mess?
It can be incomparably amazing in some moments, out of this world.
Yet, so petrifying in others.

© Edmarys Menendez ©

Why? Why? Why?

You feel small, not knowing the answer to this implausible but complex natural instinct in yourself.

It makes you feel weak, horribly weak...

You know you are strong; you know this pain will slowly drift away.

But not knowing how long it'll take, that is where you get a

sense of impatience, un-comfortableness, and a deep fear of

losing the little hope your conscious struggles to whisper at you

each day.

You do not know.

You do not know why.

You do not know why it was now.

You do not know.

What do you do?

What do you say?

Where can you go?

Who will be next if there will ever be another?

27

Live your dream and love your life

You know nothing.

You also know everything.

But you still question,

"Why?"

If Only:

It's scary not knowing whether it'll grow or if it'll crash. Yet, sometimes we know it will grow. You're on a level you've never been on and it's fascinating how distinctively amazing this level is. You cry because you're afraid but also cry because of how full of life your insides feel. It is greatly magnificent how they've done it. They have captivated your soul. **Yet, sometimes we truly believe it will grow.**

Joy...happy tears...love...

You cry as you write and no one knows how you feel. Some believe in destiny; some believe in fate and some believe in other religious beliefs. You may not know what this is at first but you do know it is beyond extraordinary. Words cannot explain how incredible you feel. It is like they´re with you at all times. Even when you're both apart you can feel their heartbeat, when you breathe you can feel their breath within yours and it hurts you to know you're both apart. At times you insanely miss that person but it's safe to say that you know they'll be back each time. You're so in love. Tears are racing towards your jawline because you have never felt so alive. Chills are all over your body.

You can sense their touch...

The future is pictured in your head and you see yourself with that significant other. You're both living together, knowing neither of you cannot bear to be apart. You have fallen completely in love with them. Their beautiful soul is divine. They are an incredible individual and you can say you're blessed that they are yours and you are there's. If and only if humans can live forever, you will be with them eternally. You love them now and always will; through thick and thin. Both bodies decaying after decades but both souls sprouting a little more each day.

"They are incredible and you're blessed to say they are yours and you are there's."

.

You Don't Deserve Me

Dishonest: That is what defines you.

Lying within each word of love you spoke.

Never understanding why my apologies were never enough.

Effortless: That was your way of showing your "support..."

Or should I say, no support at all.

No interest in my likes and passions.

Selfish: That is your kind.

Never helping me in ways that were first nature to you.

It was too much to ask for.

Empty: is your heart...a lost soul.

Removing my own from my body and being as narrow-minded
as anyone can be.

No goals, no vision, no future.

Reserved: Never showing your love to me.

Like a dead rose waiting to be cared for...

And not a rose even given.

31

Vicious: It is what you are.

Knowing what to say.

Manipulating my mind and heart.

Evaporate: It is what will happen to you.

In my mind of course...

As time passes by, I will overcome this heartbreak.

I will rejoice.

You don't deserve me.

To live is to love...

Live your dream and love your life

I Dance Alone:

I dance alone in an open space,

Each limb alive and uncontrollable.

But just one note and a smile's on my face.

A leap of freedom and then I chase,

You cannot see it; it's invisible.

I dance alone in an open space.

A feeling so deep that can replace,

An ongoing beat and I'm emotional.

But just one note and a smile's on my face.

And just in case, no matter the place,

I leave behind, something collectible.

I dance alone in an open space.

A piece of my soul, others can embrace,

A helping hand to those inconsolable.

But just one note and a smile's on my face.

It's what I live for; an act of grace,

No need for appearance, it's also spiritual.

I dance alone in an open space.

But just one note and a smile's on my face.

34   © Edmarys Menendez ©

Torn:

They were compelling,

A curious sensation,

Torn in diagonals,

In black and grey combination.

They were divergent,

To each their own story,

Like lost souls,

Damaged and gory.

But the gore isn't visible,

Only hidden in deep slits,

Like caged emotions,

Buried in bits.

I understood it all,

Like it was my own,

And like a mirror,

My reflection it shown.

The Temptation:

There was a place,

Known by few.

As "Garden of Eden,"

Created for two.

Adam was first,

An honest man.

Obeyed his God,

Since life began.

Then came Eve,

An admirable woman.

Though gullible to strangers,

Not only human.

When they met,

Love at first sight.

Cherished one another,

Day and night.

But darkness appeared,

A deceitful snake.

Skilled in persuasion,

For evil's sake.

An apple,

Chosen by it.

Had destroyed them,

Once it was bit.

It made them wiser,

The snake replied.

Yet nothing felt different,

Just guilt inside.

They admitted to God,

What they had done.

So he sent them to earth,

And their unhappiness begun.

Adam grew crops,

Every day in the sun.

While Eve gave birth,

37

Live your dream and love your life

                    To more than one.

Sunday's Alarm:

A scream across the hall.

It becomes overwhelming.

But not with conversation.

With thoughts, wandering,

Trying to figure out where to go.

Another yell.

Though, this one with words.

"Oh Meu Deus!"

Uncertain, yet I can relate.

Bilingual; Hispanic.

And it is dead.

Now, an uncommon ripple of voices resonates.

First voice still keen.

As for the other, two maybe?

A pleasurable tone; Tittering.

Exhilarated vibes seeping through their openings.

Chills.

Live your dream and love your life

A tempting infection.

My air overflowing with instant exuberance.

A trail of glee remains as it calmly fades.

And it is noon.

Seconds felt; an hour passed by.

Misty and moist.

Eyes shut and mind is elsewhere.

Disturbance gone; alarm,

Snoozed.

At The Piano:

At the piano,

It's where memorable moments are created.

At the piano,

It's where coming together is celebrated.

Loving smiles; everyone is elated.

As we sing and dance all animated.

At the piano,

We exchanged life stories; we're fascinated.

At the piano,

Each person has joined, all participated.

Husbands and wives, some not related.

But the feeling of belonging, is appreciated.

At the piano,

Every child grows well educated.

At the piano,

In every reunion, all adults are congratulated.

Some years full of tears; we compensated.

Other times in laughter; exhilarated.

© Edmarys Menendez ©   41

The Hero's Journey:

He has no words left in him.

He's been in the ocean too long.

He has failed as a hero.

He's destroyed the definition all along.

Several days in blue waters.

Deprived of nourishment.

Several times forced to stay awake.

Deprived not in abandonment.

From afar a dark boat.

A blur in his eyes.

From time to time the boat appeared.

A hand, now inside as he dries.

The old man speaks.

As he smiled and waved.

"The sea has taught us all.

As heroes are also saved."

© Edmarys Menendez ©

Monet's Pond:

Two sides.

Two sides of everything.

The left is darkness.

The right is purity.

Branches are there to reach,

Reach into the waters.

The water spreads,

As life underneath it, pushes it out.

A branch.

Its thorns.

They cut,

Deep cuts.

You bleed.

Heavily; severe.

It's out,

All out.

What's left?

The water.

Live your dream and love your life

One touch,

You're cleansed.

The pain.

It's gone.

Now piece,

It's welcoming.

As life unfolds.

Each side is released to one another.

The bad with the good.

The good with the bad.

Though it's a never-ending process,

One you cannot escape.

It starts all over,

And now the branches reach, once again.

Life is an incomplete essay, only you can control your story...

In Between:

Sometimes we're stuck. We ask ourselves, "what is our story?"
Our life is a powerful story.
Some have found their answer, others are blindly living.
It is souls like us with such incredible hearts that have such
difficulty finding our story, the story of life.
We wonder if we will ever find our story.
We are in between all the nothing and everything going on in
our hearts.
But if we give it thought, we will come to find that this in fact our
story.
This is the story of not knowing what is the story.
We share this story, our story, the story of not knowing our
story, with everyone who doesn't know what their story is either.
We also share this story with those who do have a story.
This isn't only a writing on a piece of paper.
This is where we discover how and when we help others and
ourselves.
This is the story where we find out what is the actual meaning
of life, in our lives.
That's our story.

Your Conscience:

Your conscious is an invisible box filled with infinite thoughts, feelings, perceptions, memories and much more.

It has the ability to persuade you to think in such horriific ways. Oh but that conscience of yours is much more powerful. It can eradicate the most sinful thoughts of all.

Your conscience is incomparable, unique... it is an invisible version of yourself.

If you think you cannot escape your conscious, you are wrong.

Your conscience has the ability to motivate you in the most dreadful moments in your life.

Your conscience has the power to choose what thoughts or feelings should be kept and which ones should be thrown away into the unknown.

Think positively and things will turn out great.

Think about your definition of happiness, picture it and visualize it, and it will become your reality.

Think of being that artist in front of an audience or that doctor saving lives. You will become that person you know you are capable of being and your life will be glorious.

Lover:

What is the purpose of living?
It is creating stories, discovering yourself, truly opening your heart and expanding your knowledge as you process new possibilities, lessons and obstacles.
So many of us lack greeting and smiling.
Those who lack opening their hearts are filled with loneliness, fear and rejection.
We tend to keep our voices inside us at all times.
We believe we are all different yet in some strange way, we aren't.
How is this possible?
Our expectations in life are quite similar.
We all want to be loved, to love back, find our passion, enjoy life and be happy.
But there's more.
Our most wanted similarity is actually to be accepted by others.
Yet, none of us do anything about it.
Why? We live life in fear.
What we all need to do is build courage, forget the insults and stay positive.
This way our voices can be heard and maybe we'll be able to meet some of those similar expectations.
It is quite exhausting to see how everything and everyone in the world is constantly changing.
It's like we've become coldhearted, detached and desensitized.
The worlds diversity is probably a reason why we tend to hold back.
But then again, it all comes back to fear. We're afraid of being judged or ridiculed.
We have become aliens to one another.
The only way this can be solved is to become human again.
Humanity: it is the key to everything. What exactly does that mean?

© Edmarys Menendez ©

It means being generous, compassionate, humble, trustworthy, appreciative, accepting, loyal, honest and most of all, a lover.

Learn To Move On:

Death can be stressful; it fills you with questions.
Could I have done something to make me feel better?
Could I have done something to make the other person feel better?
Was there really a possibility this person could've actually lived longer?

It is devastating when one encounters death, especially when the one who rose above you isn't an acquainted individual but someone you truly cared about and deeply loved.
Their soul remains on Earth to accompany you but it isn't enough to feel joy.
Praying, distractions, and the acceptance of the loss are not only comfortable but suitable solutions.

When emotions crowd your inner thoughts, you begin to drown in them.
Once they are released there is peace once again.
Soon after opening up and delivering a release of stress, you will begin to sense the breath of life once more.

Your mood will transform from vicious and abstruse to stormless and lucid.
It will be like eradicating the ashes from the fire in your mind.
Coping with that can be difficult indeed.
Denial steps in your life; you become adamant and refuse to believe in the truth.
When recovering and acquiring the truth, you won't let the past destroy your future.
Your spirit will affably let the other spirits in its joy and loving need.

When you accept, you will feel the love of that person who is no longer alive.

© Edmarys Menendez ©

You will feel it in both mind and soul.
Your heart will release all dark and poisoned anger and it will let in the beautiful and overflowing positive energy.
You will feel amazed and when you do, you will realize that you can finally say, "I have learned to move on."
Death is a huge barrier that is difficult for one to cope with. You will go through it and you will survive.

All you need, is patience and time.

The Thirst:

Polydipsia.
What is the best way to define that word?
It is an excessive and abnormal thirst.
Do you dance?
How many times a day do you move your body?
Do you consider yourself a dancer?
We are all dancers.
We each move our bodies over a thousand times a day.
A single gesture defines dancing.
Dance can automatically open doors, it reveals you to self-disclose yourself and feel alive.
But some of us have a stronger connection.
What connection is that exactly?
It is a connection when you first move your body in such a way, you find hidden questions in your conscious.
You say to yourself, "Why am I so nervous?
Is it because I am afraid to embarrass myself in front of an audience?
Or am I afraid to feel like a failure, a weak and lonely individual?
Is this it? Is this the moment I finally realize where I stand in my life?
Does this determine my future?
Will this become a memory or an everyday lifestyle?"
In that split-second when the music starts playing, the lights fade and the audience gazes all attention on the stage, your mindset will suddenly shift to a different world.
So you dance; you role, you jump, you walk, you reach, you give it your all.
Your energy is fading and so is the song and the dance piece has ended.
As the crowd cheers and you bow for applause, the missing puzzle piece is fully placed.
Your true self is no longer hidden.

© Edmarys Menendez ©

You are a dancer, an entertainer, a giver.
You are out of breath, in need of water.
As the crowd rises, you then realize your thirst isn't for water, it is for life.
It is the greatest, powerful and most unforgettable moment.
This day will forever remain in your mind and heart.
You will carry it throughout your life in order to live each day exactly how you are supposed to live it. Why is that?
This encounter to dance has prepared you for challenges in the future.
Life will push you in every direction.
Yet, this first experience with dance was the push you needed.
Now, you are forever thirsty, in need of life, and you are ready.

Distinctiveness:

Some of us believe all humans are different. Some believe all humans are the same. Both answers are correct. We are one, with distinctive qualities, likes and dislikes. It is with all those different aspects where we all come together to create something beautiful. As lovers of this world, we should all try to understand others. Once we do, no matter what opinions are being said or acted upon, we end up appreciating everything and everyone a bit more.

Do you see yourself the same as everyone else? Everyone is unique and has different personality traits that make up who they are. Although, with social norms now a day, you might see yourself falling into a robotic lifestyle where fashion, music and celebrities are depicted as something to follow. Society and social norms persuade and train our minds to think a certain way. As this happens, we weaken ourselves into becoming someone we are not. Our distinctiveness becomes transparent and within time will vanish. It is our decision to build courage and destroy these norms. Once that is done, our unique qualities, likes, dislikes and creativity will shine from our spirits naturally.

What makes you unique? The fact that we make our own decisions is what makes us unique. People have similar characteristics but different reasons behind each decision. Accept, don't judge. We've all lived through certain obstacles, challenges and life lessons creating those pathways to our future. Not everyone can handle life changing decisions the same way. In order to accept and appreciate their choices, we need to listen and understand first.

© Edmarys Menendez ©

How can you still be yourself when others think differenlty around you? Being true to yourself and to others is what makes us humans such extraordinary creatures. That is the beauty of us all. Be true to yourself and to others. Those unique qualities are who you are. We all have weak traits, those traits that give you depression; but those are the traits that teach you life lessons and make you stronger. These questions may have a plethora of answers. Each answer with its own story, its own reason.

Distinctiveness has its positive and negative outcomes. If we get stuck along the way, life will control you. If you free your true essence, you will control life.This is where we create beauty, the beauty of being human, being imperfectly perfect. We are the masterpieces in our lives.

The Hidden Soul:

You awaken from a deep sleep. Your body is crying and yelling your name while thanking you. You feel alive and you have fully awoken. When you are still, your physical self speaks to you and says you have given it life and when you move, it says you have given it freedom. Every inch of your body feels full and every time it loses strength, you feed it more and eliminate its emptiness. These are the moments you cherish. Your soul is beyond happy. Who is your soul? It is the one who hides beneath you. You nurture yourself with what you desire and your happiness is your self-realization.

This desire searches for your soul every second it can and reaches your heart. In order for you to feel like your true self, you have to let it speak. You have to listen to it, grab it, and feel it. This desire is you and you are it. It completes you and it is it your breath. It has been by your side your entire life to support you and has given you a hand when you have felt alone or out of place. It is how you communicate with others. It expresses what you feel in such a unique and incredible way.

You never noticed how much this desire was a part of your life until today. You may have been scared of showing others. Yet, when this desire is free, your soul is free. You may feel out of place, not knowing where to go if it wasn't for it. Confusion and other's opinions interfere with your thoughts. Then you hide who you are in fear. Is it difficult to find one's true self? Yes; it takes time, courage, and self-motivation. Most of us have not yet fully recognized our true self but this desire of life, of living, will save you.

© Edmarys Menendez ©

Do you remember the first time you let that desire escape? Maybe it wasn't completely free. Maybe it just saw its reflection in the mirror. That was the day you realized it needs you and you need it. After this experiment or slip away, your heart will create a desire of its own and it will feel magical. How is that so? Everyone's desire to live has been part of our developement inside our mother's womb. Life distractions can be misleading. Depression, hurt, loss, loneliness...they persuade us to hide away forever. That day your desire to live showed itself again; you knew it was calling. Now you must learn to let go of it all.

Doesn't matter what mistakes you have made or what mistakes you're going to make. Your'e living now and think of nothing. You have no worries and your body moves itself to where it wants to go. Yes, you will surprise yourself each time and you will notice what your soul is capable of. You will encounter new barriers every sunrise. That desire to live will surely rise above it all.

You might ask yourself numerous times the same questions. What is my purpose? What is my calling? Who am I? You are the leader of your future. The one God has chosen you to be. Years will pass and life will be exquisite, exciting and filled with accomplishments.

This desire is everything you need and it is everywhere you go. It surrounds each and every one of us. But it does not suffocate. It lets you breathe; you feel free. Free because it lets you be you. If you want to yell, you yell, if you want to cry, you cry, if you want to laugh, you laugh... The desire to live frees all of your emotions without hesitation.

© Edmarys Menendez ©   57

Our thoughts are filled with so much of what others say and not of what we know... The combination of these thoughts leads us all to believe who we think we are and not who we truly are. When you let these thoughts overpower your inner self, your soul will be in another body, another mind, another face and another person; not where it should belong.

We all need this desire to live in order to feel alive. If we live without it, our physical and mental state will weaken. That is not who we are. Let it move you. You can let go of all that weighs you down and you can open the doors to a brighter future, a successful life. Wanting to live and not just wanting to exist. This is where you can be yourself. This is where you can achieve your goals. Nothing can interfere.

We all struggle when we feel lost, we feel broken, alone in the world. The solution is to simply believe, have that desire to live, to be limitless. Listen to your inner self, it speaks honesty. Don't let it hide, let it fly and feel alive. It will take time.

Patience is all you need. It is the key to encounter the path of self-realization. Block the loud silence of the world and listen to the whispers of your soul. When you hear that desire calling your name, welcome it with open arms. Then and only then, will you will be free; truly alive. The desire to live, that is your path. Follow the trail.

© Edmarys Menendez ©

Love moves us,

but does not control us...

Rise:

Mixed emotions are caged inside your ribs. Their smile is contagious, a simple gesture that captivates. But this feeling has been lost. You don't know where it has gone. You miss their presence, their touch, their sweetness, their smile, their eyes, you miss them whole. A heavy heart is what you now carry. It has excessively bled. You are weak and in no control. It is something incomparably exceptional. Just this morning you wore that lost smile and it was amazing. You have opened the doors to your lost soul and it is home once again.

As you inhale, your insides twist and turn as a reminder of their absence. When you exhale, all negative emotions triggered are released into the air of lost souls. You were there not so long ago. This heart of yours is no longer lost and it has repaired itself with marvelous energy. You have deja vu numerous times throughout the week where it triggers membranes with overjoyed and unforgettable memories with that person. Certain clips play in your thoughts and you realize, there's no need in suffering.

Your mind is powerful. A fearless conscious decision is what persuades you in believing you are strong. Yes, you are. There's no need to search for another damaged soul. A fully rejoiced soul will find you instead. That other individual will be an extra piece who will eventually just appear in the rarest moments. No matter what outside sources say or do, you have the power to control what you think, say, and do. You are unstoppable. So open that cage and rise bird, fly as high as you can.

Third Love:

Third time's the charm, or so they say. It's not precise. Who's to say your true love isn't your first or your 15th? Love is strange and it is not planned. It has many depths and many versions. We don't all experience the same type of love. If you experienced the lighthearted love, this is the one that has rarely disagreements, rarely any fights. It is all smile and laughter. It is pure and has no intention of hurting your heart but it lacks passion...It isn't real enough.

There's the adventure love, that's the one that drives you crazy...the good crazy. Fondling and making love everywhere and anywhere... the love that wipes your innocense goodbye. Lust overpowers both humans and there are no limits...no rules. It is tempting but it can become exhausting over time.

Heartache love is another. It wants you there at all times with no excuses and craves you every second of every day but it is selfish...only wanting you for their needs, not caring for yours at all. Your passions, your goals, your vision... they aren't important. They want your support but won't give you the same amount back. They want your attention but won't give you the same amount back. They want your entire heart but they won't give you the same amount back.

How about the play it safe love? This one has no boundaries. It is there for you at all times and it is everything you wanted but for some odd reason, you don't feel it. No matter how great they may seem, you stay because you fear the loneliness, you fear not being cared for or not having someone to lean on, so you play it safe and stay.

Then there's the true love, the one we all dream of. It is the love we think of day and night. It exists and sometimes it may even be right in front of us, but the other types of love distract us...

61

they blur our vision. True love will love you and support you unconditionally but will bluntly tell you when you're wrong... not to hurt you, but to teach you, to guide you, to push your limits, break you to make you and most of all, to really and truly love you. Many of us have experienced many of these types of love in some way or another. Some have found their true love and lost them, some are with them now. Some may even get to say, third time's the charm and others may not. Love is strange, it has many depths and many versions...but it is wonderful. It is magical. It is impossible to live without.

Hopeless Romantic:

It's not the money.
It's deeper than that; beneath the souls where the hearts are reborn.
Those fancy nights, the red petals, a higher level in our spirits... we all want that.
We aim for that kind of love, a beautiful and unique way of living life.
Those warm mornings, the white backgrounds, a pure glorified touch from within, we crave that. Some of us have refused to accept it, while others nearly die for it.
It is so powerful it can drive our minds to wander in an unknown dimension.
Endless cries roar and you've not yet found this missing piece.
No, it is not a piece you're missing but your other half.
Curious...lost...scared.
Where are you? How long will it be? It mocks you everywhere you go and everywhere you are. It's so lovely, so ravishing and so delightful.
Every time you search, it has a way of hiding. It breaks you.
When will they come? You don't know and you don't want to wait.
You cannot breathe, you grow impatient.
How can others avoid it? How can they live without it?
There are different versions , different paths... Which one do you take?
You have yet to obtain that love of highest power.
It is the one thing that turns your insdes into ways you can't explain.
There is no care in the world because it shuts you out of all horrifying realities.

It is so magical that those realities become fantasies and your created world becomes the hidden truth. How could you know all this if you have not yet found it yourself?
That is something you do not know.
All you know, is once it reveals itself to you, it will surely feel the same as you. It will stay for eternity until time no longer exists, until there is nothing.
When will that be? You don't know but it will happen, or will it? How do you know the future is not a liar? You don't know that either.
It is those mysteries that leave your mind blown with infinite microscopic truths, impossibly unable to reach unless they are welcomed.
It is in fact the mystery of all.
Deep inside you know we all have a need for it but some of us are insanely obsessed in finding it. Time; it all comes down to the hours, the minutes and the unnoticed seconds.
That moment you find it, your life will finally begin.
The life you live now is preparing you for that special moment.
Excited, impatient, nervous...
It will come, it will be divine, it will be love.

Motherly Hand:

A mother's hand is indeed a special one.
We should cherish it, protect it and love it as much as it does to us...or even more.
It has made you who you are today. It held you when you first saw light.
It's protected you from that moment on. It has taught you to forgive, love and care and has supported you through times of confusion and overwhelmed stages in life.
It is tender and influencing in ways that you yourself cannot comprehend...
Until years pass and understand its hard work and judgement.
Every day you see light again, thanks to this hand, your mother's hand.
You realize how thankful you are.
This hand belongs to your mother who has taught you the right way of life with long educational talks all these years.
Words of wisdom have been spoken so you can reach your fullest potential.
It is a helping hand, a loving hand, an irreplaceable hand...
Without this extraordinary hand, you wouldn't have been able to live such an honorable life with someone there to hold you and guide you.
It is immensely appreciated each day.
This hand is unique.
Sometimes with a fresh manicure and other times in real need of one.
Its creases and lines defining it's diligence.
Always comforting, always affectionate and devoted to your happiness and success.
This is the hand we must keep in our hearts forever.
This is the hand we must work hard for, to give it everything it deserves.

Not only has this hand been with you since you first opened your eyes but it will be with you until you close them forevermore inside your heart, your mind and memories... Give this hand your all for it is your mother's hand who will never fail nor ridicule you.
Thank you hand, you are my life, you are my everything.
Thank you mom, you are my life, you are my everything.

Self-Love:

A reflection in a mirror isn't exactly a suitable definition to who you are.
It is beyond the reflection where you see your true self.
A mirror is a powerful tool where you can examine your identity, values and even your life's greatest decisions.
It is an applicable tool that can be used in our daily lives.
From the minute we wake up to the minute we fall asleep.
It is a guide.
To some, a mirror shows a simple reflection, to others it is deeper than that.
If you believe it is more than a face, then this belief says you are a seeker in meanings; a curious individual.
You like to know what is behind the masks and armor.
It is the strongest and most invisible trait you can carry.
Because of your curiosity and fearlessness in such things, you will surpass a plethora of unbearable troubles as you have in the past, present and will pass in the future.
Some say you may give too much of yourself to others, but it is because of that, you are willing to let go of all hatred and jealousy in the world, especially in times of despair and hungriness.
You love who you are as an individual and you're determined in not changing.
You are beyond satisfied for who you have become as a whole and as you grow and keep learning from not only yourself but from others.
Life can surprise you but you know you have the power to choose how you want to live the rest of your life.
You are unstoppable.
You are love. You are loved.
Self-love.

The Art Within:

What is art? Can it be ignored? Does it mean the same to all?
Art is life, it is love, it is beauty.
It can mean the world to some and nothing to others.
But art is everything. It is beautifully incomparable.
It's part of living.
Why live without painters, poets, dancers, singers, musicians or actors?
Why settle for such a dull life?
No excitment, no thrill, no exhilaration.
Art moves us in such ways that cannot be expressed in words.
Words aren't enough.
Art is everywhere...it lives inside us.
From the waves we hear clashing to the shore to a single stroke of a paintbrush on a canvas.
Art is happiness.
It is also rage and sorrow.
Art is how we express our emotions.
Dancing with a lover or dancing because it lifts our souls.
Singing to a relative or singing because it gives us hope.
Painting for oneself because it calms our spirits.
Art is astonishing.
Art is radical.
Art is tremendous.
Be art, use art, love art.
From the second you open your eyes each day, to the moment you have them shut.
Art is life, it is love, it is beauty.
Love art, it loves you back.

Love is Life:

Why do we love? Some believe it's useless.
We all die anyway.
But who's to say we do not love beyond that?
Reincarnation?
Heaven?
Hell?
Love is life,
It is everything.
You can't live without love; that's not living.
Love is unique and complex.
How we love and how we are loved can be completely different.
Loving your mother or father or sibling are all different types of love.
How you loved your first partner and how you love your current or your future partner is also different.
Yet, loving is how we stay sane.
Love is the reason we cross mountains and move souls.
From sending letters to surprise visits...that is the life.
That is the life we all need. A life filled with love all around.
Deep connections, wise chats, an ongoing learning adventure...
To love is to live.
Do you want to keep living?
Do you want to truly live?
Then love as hard as you can.
No limits, no boundaries, no hesitations...
Because loving unconditionally is a life worth living.

Live your dream and love your life

Acknowledgements:

I want to thank everyone who supported me and those who encouraged me in finishing and publishing my first book. I have had magnificent teachers thus far from education to my household. I have had an incredible journey writing this anthology. I've learned to appreciate every spec of existence, to love and take nothing for granted. We have to be thankful for what we have in order to help others with what they don't have.

We are humans and we all make mistakes. There are times we think poorly and make horrible decisions. The solution is simple. It is the kindness we give to others in order to receive the same back. Live with a pure heart. Kindness is the first step of acceptance. Sharing love and compassion is what brings us all together. When serving others, we receive a fulfillment of happiness. In fact, happiness is our true essence, even if we think not.

Despite all the negative barriers we encounter, underneath it all, we have the need to love, care, and appreciate. It is when we don't receive it all back that has an effect in our emotions. Why waste our time with all of that, when we can use our life exploring life itself? Nature speaks in a language we cannot comprehend. Our earth is beautiful and everything in it as well. It is our home and we should all protect it and care for it. We are connected with it all.

Our minds are functioned to act with contradictions and questions. However, no one wants to feel afraid or unsure. Even when our bodies are still, our minds stay active. When we fear, it can be powerful, controlling and can turn into an ongoing thought. There is no need to think negatively. We are never alone. God is with us at all times.

When nothing can possibly guide you, life encounters will. When everything is dark and seems impossible, belief and

70   © Edmarys Menendez ©

confidence will bring you light. Once all negativity vanishes, everything will be possible. When reaching a goal or striving for something you want to succeed in, it can be challenging and ignoring all distractions is the most difficult.

Our minds change our bodies and our bodies change our minds too. Your body can shape who you are mentally. Finding out your path, your wants, your goals, your passions etc. is a long journey. Everyone's thoughts are filled with compliments, opinions and thougts from other individuals. Yet, that is not what defines you.

On the contrary, there is actually something deeper in us than just thought and emotion. As a child, your brain has not yet started conceptual thought. As you get older, you become an open basket as you fill it with experiences. The past are memories, the now carries a pen and the future is an infinite paper that is filled with unanswered questions from the answers we choose in the now. Our presence is enough; nothing needs to be added to who you are already.

This is the beauty of oneself. It takes time and experience to find your true self. It can get tiring but that persistency will be worth it. Our calling is a gift to be received from our voices within and that is what we listen to. I consider myself an encourager of life. I can truly say I am a young woman with the desire to live and encourage others to live as well. I thank those who've been there from the start. They have all been incredible and loving human beings. If you're reading this, you are also wonderful. Thank you for reading my book.